THE BODY POSITIVITY JOURNAL

The Body Positivity Journal

Inspirational Prompts and Practices to Boost Self-Love and Acceptance

MEGHAN SYLVESTER

ROCKRIDGE PRESS

Cover and Interior Designer: Lisa Forde
Art Producer: Janice Ackerman
Editor: Nora Spiegel
Production Editor: Melissa Edeburn
Production Manager: Martin Worthington
Illustration courtesy of Creative Market.
Author photo courtesy of Cynthia Alexandra.

Paperback ISBN: Print 978-1-63807-075-7
R0

This Journal Belongs to

_____

Contents

Introduction

ALL BODIES ARE GOOD BODIES.

Bodies of all ages, shapes, sizes, and colors are worthy of being honored and celebrated. People of all abilities, genders, and orientations are deserving of support and love. Yet every day, people all over the world wake up wishing their bodies were different. An unrelenting pressure to look a certain way has left many feeling insecure about their bodies. Why do impossible beauty standards exist when most of the world doesn't fit the mold?

We are bombarded with toxic messaging about our bodies from every angle. Mass media, diet companies, and the billion-dollar beauty industry profit from the insecurities they perpetuate. From an early age we pick up on critical messages about our bodies in family conversations, the doctor's office, and the schoolyard. Everywhere we look, something or someone is touting a particular body shape while shaming another.

The good news? More and more people are embarking on a path of body acceptance—*people just like you*. As you journey into your unique world of body perception, you will find you have the power to uncouple yourself from the old, exhausting narratives that leave you feeling like there's got to be another way. It just takes some time and commitment.

Fat acceptance can be credited as the catalyst for the body positive movement. In 1969, after witnessing the unfair treatment of his wife because of her size, Bill Fabrey rallied allies and activists and formed an organization known today as the National Association to Advance Fat Acceptance (NAAFA). As the movement grew, people of color were not receiving representation and support equal to their white counterparts. This disparity gave rise to the feminist group The Fat Underground. In 1973, they published a manifesto that targeted diet culture and beauty industries, calling for "equal rights for fat people."

In the 1990s, The Body Positive was founded as a support system for those struggling with body-image issues due to toxic societal messaging. By the 2000s, influencers and celebrities, most of whom were plus-size Black women, were at the forefront of initiating the body positive conversation on social media. What started out as a stand for fat acceptance has now led to the call for equal rights, representation, and reverence for all bodies.

The body positive movement still has a long way to go, in particular when it comes to representation of disabled people and LGBTQIA+ people (especially transgender and nonbinary individuals). Another issue is that the plus-size bodies highlighted in the media still tend to conform to idealized, cisgender, and Eurocentric beauty standards—for instance, hourglass figures, "perfect" skin—marginalizing bodies that don't fit those standards. For all the good it has done, some critique the body positive movement for placing the body at the center of the human experience. Some people prefer a more neutral approach when it comes to their bodies, which alleviates any pressure to love the body or think of it in a positive (or negative) light. As the movement evolves, we can only hope the day will come when humans are as celebrated for what's on the inside. We are all worthy of love, happiness, and abundance simply because we exist.

As for my story, I was born with a birthmark in the middle of my upper lip. For years, feelings of shame and embarrassment led to a lacking sense of self-worth. I struggled with a crushing fear of rejection and a lurking sense of doom that I would be "found out." These fears later manifested as perfectionism, people pleasing, and hypercriticism about the rest of my body. (Sound familiar?) The constant need to prove I was good enough was exhausting and brought me to the brink of a mental breakdown. After my physical health took a turn for the worse, I embarked on a quest of healing and self-discovery. Eventually, I realized how much my toxic body perception was sucking the joy out of life. After the birth of my third child, I was called once again to examine the judgments I held against myself. Why had weight gain and saggy skin made me feel so unworthy? As a mentor who is trained in positive psychology, I realized how not okay this was for my well-being and vowed to dive deeper into my journey of body consciousness. This path led me to the work I do today as an advocate for body acceptance and empowerment.

My mission as a kundalini yoga, meditation, and mindfulness teacher is to help others find true fulfillment by releasing insecurities and tuning in to joy. I have guided students all over the globe through positive transformational shifts, and it's my honor to bring this work to you now. Through prompts, exercises, and positive affirmations, this journal will compassionately guide you along a path that will teach you how to honor your body, transmuting negative self-perceptions into body acceptance and self-love. There will be a few exercises centered around mindful movement and gentle breath. Modifications are suggested for all abilities, but please tune in to the wisdom of your own body and modify in ways that feel supportive for you.

Though this journal is a wonderful supplement to your healing journey, it should not replace professional treatment. If you are currently under the care of a professional, please continue. A resource list of treatment options is included at the back of this journal. If you're trans and/or nonbinary, know that the steps you take toward affirming your body and these body positive prompts and exercises can coexist. And for anyone reading this, however you identify, please go about this journal in kindness to yourself, and remember that only you get to decide what to do with your body, whether that's accepting it as it is or accepting that you may want to change it.

Positive body image isn't a final destination but a journey, one of self-acceptance composed of conscious daily decisions and a commitment to a greater awareness of why one feels as one does. Though the journey may be difficult at times, know that finding liberation from body dissatisfaction is possible.

Thank you for picking up this journal and committing to doing the work. The world needs you! Let's get started.

YOU HAVE BEEN
CRITICIZING YOURSELF
FOR YEARS AND IT
HASN'T WORKED.
TRY APPROVING OF
YOURSELF AND SEE
WHAT HAPPENS.

—Louise Hay

Unpacking Your Relationship with Your Body

We aren't born begrudging our bodies. But somewhere along the way, we learn that our worth is tied to our appearance. We learn to hide the parts of ourselves that don't quite fit in, and we grow more shameful and suppressed. The good news? If we can learn body dissatisfaction, then we can unlearn it! We can build healthy relationships with our bodies that do not dismiss or discount our true feelings. In this section you'll have the opportunity to explore the negative thoughts swirling around your mind and where they came from. It's time to kick off your journey by shining a light on the source of your negative body image.

Create Your Sacred Space

Designating a particular area of your home to your healing journey can enhance your experience. It doesn't have to be fancy. It can be a dish set in a corner, or a small section of a console or nightstand. Now, find a place that feels peaceful and serene, and create your sacred space. Adorn it with items from nature like feathers, rocks, and flowers. Add pictures, candles, or anything else that makes you feel connected and inspired. Of course, you can work through this journal anywhere—it's just nice to have a dedicated space! Add to it and change it as your energy evolves. Use the space below to write three to five words that describe how you'd like to feel when you visit your sacred space.

_____

_____

_____

_____

_____

Let's start by getting clear on your big "why." Why does learning how to embrace your body feel especially important to you at this moment in your life? Why is an unhealthy relationship with your body no longer an option?

_____

_____

_____

_____

_____

_____

_____

_____

_____

_____

_____

_____

_____

_____

You weren't born thinking negatively about your body. What is an early childhood memory of an incident that caused you to feel insecure about your body or made you realize that something didn't feel right or aligned? Paint the scene: Where were you, who were you with, and what happened? How did it make you feel?

_____

_____

_____

_____

_____

_____

_____

_____

_____

_____

_____

_____

_____

I HAVE THE POWER TO OUTGROW BELIEFS THAT NO LONGER SERVE ME.

Let It All Out!

Get negative thoughts out of your head and onto paper. Let it all out! On a separate piece of paper, write down the top 10 complaints you have about your body. This might not feel good, although it may also feel a little cathartic! Once you're done, safely and ceremoniously dispose of this list, by either burning, burying, or flushing it. Then, in the box provided, write this healing statement: "I forgive you, I release you, I am moving forward."

Unpack your feelings around food by talking about it as though it were an acquaintance. How would you describe your relationship? How does it feel when you and food get together—easy or tense? Are you accepting of one another?

_____

_____

_____

_____

_____

_____

_____

_____

_____

_____

_____

_____

_____

_____

Recall a memory from your younger years when either you, a friend, or a family member was celebrated or praised for losing weight or conforming to a certain beauty ideal. How do you think this experience impacted your feelings around self-worth and body image?

_____

_____

_____

_____

_____

_____

_____

_____

_____

_____

_____

_____

_____

_____

FINDING LOVE AND ACCEPTANCE FOR MY BODY BEGAN TO SHIFT THE MOMENT I STARTED TO PAY ATTENTION TO THE RELATIONSHIP I HAVE WITH MYSELF. OF COURSE, THERE WILL ALWAYS BE MOMENTS WHEN IT'S HARD TO EMBODY SELF-ACCEPTANCE, BUT COMFORTING OURSELVES IS A LIFE-ALTERING EXPERIENCE. WHAT PUT EVERYTHING IN PER-SPECTIVE WAS BEING REMINDED THAT MY LEGACY ON THIS EARTH IS HOW I IMPACT PEOPLE'S LIVES, NOT HOW I LOOK. CONSIDER HOW YOU CAN IMPACT YOUR OWN LIFE. LOVE YOURSELF NOW—IF NOT, WHEN?!? NOW IS THE PERFECT OPPORTUNITY! JUST LIKE THE EARTH GOES THROUGH SEA-SONS, OUR BODY DOES, TOO, SO HONOR IT! IT'S SUCH A SACRED VESSEL.

— *Fonzy*

Ego Eradicator

Ego Eradicator is a kundalini exercise that helps you bust through negative, fear-based thinking and unsupportive habits. Try it now:

1. Come to a comfortable seated position, either cross-legged or in a chair, with your feet planted firmly on the ground.

2. Make your hands into fists, then point your thumbs up. Raise your arms so that you create a V around your head. (If this is not available to you, simply close your eyes and visualize—visualization is just as potent!)

3. Close your eyes and begin breath of fire: a quick breath through the nose activated at the navel center. It's similar to a dog panting but with a closed mouth and breath through the nose.

4. Do this for two to three minutes.

Tip: Do the exercise while listening to a powerful song for an enhanced experience! Immediately after completion, write the top five thoughts and/or habits you are ready to bust through.

_____

_____

_____

_____

_____

Do you feel like you have to hide or change your true nature to fit in? For some it may be restricting food to look a certain way; for others it could be dressing in a way that doesn't feel authentic in order to be accepted. What tactics have you adopted to conceal or alter your true nature? How is this impacting your happiness today?

_____

_____

_____

_____

_____

_____

_____

_____

_____

_____

_____

_____

_____

_____

_____

_____

Reflect on a time when you recently had to get dressed for a specific occasion, such as a party, work event, or outing. How would you like the experience of getting dressed to feel, and what's stopping you from feeling that way now?

_____

_____

_____

_____

_____

_____

_____

_____

_____

_____

_____

_____

_____

Was a positive body image modeled for you as a child or teenager? Did you ever hear the adults around you speaking kindly about their bodies or dressing in a way that reflected their true nature regardless of societal expectations? If you had to model a positive body image to your younger self, what kinds of things would you do and say?

_____

_____

_____

_____

_____

_____

_____

_____

_____

_____

_____

_____

_____

FOR YEARS, I THOUGHT MY FRUSTRATION AND UNHAPPINESS STEMMED FROM THE FACT THAT I WAS FAT. I THOUGHT IF I COULD JUST LOSE WEIGHT, THEN I'D BE HAPPIER AND I'D LOVE MY JOB MORE AND ALL MY RELATIONSHIPS WOULD PROBABLY IMPROVE. AT THE TIME, I WAS WEIGHING MYSELF MULTIPLE TIMES A DAY. IT WAS OBSESSIVE AND CRUEL AND NOT CONDUCIVE TO HAPPINESS. MY JOURNEY OF BODY ACCEPTANCE FINALLY HELPED ME ESCAPE THAT LIFE. I'VE REALIZED THAT HAPPINESS IS NOT YOUR WEIGHT; IT'S A DECISION THAT ONLY I GET TO MAKE. NOT ONLY HAVE I SUCCEEDED AND MADE HUGE ACCOMPLISHMENTS AT WORK AND IN MY RELATIONSHIPS AS A RESULT OF THIS WORK, BUT I LOVE MYSELF—LIKE, REALLY AND TRULY LOVE MYSELF.

—*Angela*

Do you measure the success of movement by calories burned or muscles built or by how you feel? Historically, have you been able to experience exercise as a joyful activity? What mindset shift around movement and exercise would you like to make for it to become a more pleasurable experience?

_____

_____

_____

_____

_____

_____

_____

_____

_____

_____

_____

_____

_____

_____

_____

As a child, did you ever try to conceal, camouflage, or alter your appearance or particular body parts with clothing, makeup, or something else? Why did that feel important to you? How do you feel this has shaped you today? Does it feel good or restrictive?

_____

_____

_____

_____

_____

_____

_____

_____

_____

_____

_____

_____

_____

Reflect on your main childhood insecurities about your body. You are invited now to gently begin the process of releasing these thoughts by finishing this declaration: "Dear Insecurity, thank you for trying to keep me safe, but I no longer need you. I'm ready to release you because . . ."

_____

_____

_____

_____

_____

_____

_____

_____

_____

_____

_____

_____

_____

Loving Your Inner Child

Sending love to your inner child is a beautiful tool for releasing wounds of the past. Find a picture of yourself from childhood. If you can't find one, just draw a figure that represents your younger self—a stick figure is fine! Play some beautiful music and create a rhythm of long, slow, deep breaths. As you gaze at your picture, silently begin repeating the words "You are worthy, you are wonderful, you are whole." Do this for as long as you need to feel the words coming to life in your mind, body, and soul. Afterward, in the space provided, reflect on the words you most wanted to hear as a child. Then, jot down three kind things you'd like to tell yourself every day.

_____

_____

_____

_____

_____

Imagine traveling back in time and hearing your younger self speak negatively about their body. What would you say in response to lift their spirits? How would you encourage and support this sweet child to think more kindly about their body?

_____

_____

_____

_____

_____

_____

_____

_____

_____

_____

_____

_____

_____

_____

Think of a time you felt really proud of your body. What happened and how did it make you feel? What can you do to experience this feeling again?

_____

_____

_____

_____

_____

_____

_____

_____

_____

_____

_____

_____

Who profits from your insecurities and benefits from your negative body perception? If you sat down with the CEOs of the diet and beauty industries, what types of things would you share with them about how they negatively impact people's lives with their messaging?

_____

_____

_____

_____

_____

_____

_____

_____

_____

_____

_____

_____

_____

_____

I AM LEARNING HOW TO FIND JOY WITHIN MY BODY.

Who from your childhood had the biggest impact on the way you think about food and eating? What kinds of things did you learn about food from this person? Were they positive, negative, or somewhere in between?

_____

_____

_____

_____

_____

_____

_____

_____

_____

_____

_____

_____

_____

_____

How will having a positive body image change the rest of your life? How will it impact the other facets of your life, such as health, success, relationships, and more?

_____

_____

_____

_____

_____

_____

_____

_____

_____

_____

_____

_____

_____

_____

Positive Affirmations

By mindfully shifting the thoughts and words you choose, your brain will begin to positively reorganize itself through a phenomenon called neuroplasticity. Pretty cool, right? Positive affirmations create new, positive stimuli for your brain and serve as a wonderful support to promote a greater sense of fulfillment. An easy way to write an affirmation is to use the words "I am" followed by an attribute you'd like to step into more fully. For example: "I am healthy and full of vitality." In the space provided, write three to five of your own positive affirmations. Next, write your affirmations on sticky notes or index cards, and place them in locations where you usually fall into a pattern of negative self-talk (e.g., by the mirror or next to the refrigerator). This will help your brain rewire old patterns and cultivate a more positive outlook.

I am _____.

I am _____.

I am _____.

I am _____.

I am _____.

ONE DAY I DECIDED THAT
I WAS BEAUTIFUL, AND SO I
CARRIED OUT MY LIFE AS IF
I WAS A BEAUTIFUL GIRL . . .
IT DOESN'T HAVE ANYTHING
TO DO WITH HOW THE WORLD
PERCEIVES YOU. WHAT
MATTERS IS WHAT YOU SEE.

— *Gabourey Sidibe*

Reevaluating Outside Influences on Your Body

We continuously receive messages from the media, our family and friends, and the culture at large about how we should look, dress, and act if we want to fit in. Eventually, we begin to believe these messages, and they become part of our story. These beliefs take hold and direct the way we think and speak to ourselves. This restrictive way of thinking has caused so many to feel insecure or shameful about their appearance. But it doesn't have to be this way. What if you were able to uncouple yourself from these beliefs and write your own story? Understanding why you think the way you do empowers you to decide if certain stories and beliefs are actually serving you or instead are stopping you from living a life that feels good. Are you ready to wipe the slate clean?

Consumption Clean-Up

The media you consume impacts your mental and emotional well-being just as much as the food you consume impacts your physical wellness. Think about the information you take in: Does it promote a healthy body image? This information can be anything from social media accounts to publications and programming, like movies, podcasts, and TV shows. Think about the brands you buy and the musical artists you listen to. Do they support a positive body image or an impossible beauty standard? Write down how you want your media consumption to make you feel. Next, create a list of any brands, media, or other outlets that you are ready to remove from your life. Finally, research a few different outlets that support a healthy body image and provide inspiration, and record them here.

_____

_____

_____

_____

_____

_____

_____

_____

_____

_____

Where are you right now when it comes to body acceptance: love, like, neutral, shame, or somewhere else? Where do you want to be? A gentle reminder: Wherever you are is okay.

_____

_____

_____

_____

_____

_____

_____

_____

_____

_____

_____

_____

_____

Who were the beauty icons you admired or looked up to during your childhood and formative years? How did their body types influence the way you thought and felt about your body?

_____

_____

_____

_____

_____

_____

_____

_____

_____

_____

_____

_____

_____

_____

Reflect on your family's beliefs around bodies. Were certain body types, like athletic, thin, or curvy, held up as the ideal? Were other kinds of bodies dismissed as unnatural or undesirable? How did your caregivers talk about their own bodies? Were those closest to you always chasing a certain body shape and size?

_____

_____

_____

_____

_____

_____

_____

_____

_____

_____

_____

_____

_____

_____

_____

I ENJOY TREATING MY BODY WITH KINDNESS AND RESPECT THROUGH MY THOUGHTS, ACTIONS, AND WORDS.

When you were growing up, were there any rules or expectations around food, movement, or enhancing your body that didn't feel right to you? Are you still implementing similar rules? How do these expectations make you feel?

_____

_____

_____

_____

_____

_____

_____

_____

_____

_____

_____

_____

_____

_____

_____

Were any friends or classmates celebrated because of their physical appearance or how they dressed? Did the desire to fit a particular standard breed any negative feelings within you, like competition, self-doubt, or constant comparison? How have these feelings impacted how you operate in the world today?

_____

_____

_____

_____

_____

_____

_____

_____

_____

_____

_____

_____

_____

IN MY 20S, MY RELATIONSHIP TO MY BODY WAS VERY AES-
THETIC. IT WAS ROOTED IN HOW I LOOKED TO OTHERS, HOW
ATTRACTIVE I COULD BE CONSIDERED, AND MY SENSE OF SELF
WAS VERY MUCH TIED UP IN THAT EXTERNAL VALIDATION. NOW
IN MY LATE 30S, I MARVEL AT WHAT MY BODY CAN DO. I NO
LONGER LOOK AT MYSELF AS THIS PRETTY OBJECT ON DIS-
PLAY FOR OTHERS—INSTEAD, MY RELATIONSHIP TO MY BODY
IS ROOTED IN ITS INCREDIBLE CAPACITY TO MOVE, BREATHE,
AND CARRY ME THROUGH MY DAYS. AT 36 I CAN DO THINGS
I COULDN'T DO IN MY 20S. I AM STRONG AND HEALTHY, AND
THAT MAKES ME FEEL BEAUTIFUL AND POWERFUL.

— *Camila*

Pause, Ask, Reframe

Cognitive reframing is used by therapists to help clients perceive an experience through a more empowered lens. In this exercise you will learn a body positive version of this technique, promoting a healthier self-image. Here's how:

1. **Pause:** When an unkind thought about your body crosses your mind, get into the habit of pausing by taking a deep breath. This will give you space to respond with a healthy shift.

2. **Ask:** Is this thought serving me?

3. **Reframe:** Instead of complaining, what can you be grateful for about your body in this moment?

Your turn: In the space provided, write a negative thought you recently had about your body. Then, practice this technique. Record your thoughts below as you move through each step. Once you do this enough, your mind will naturally lean toward gratitude while releasing old, unhealthy narratives.

_____

_____

_____

_____

_____

_____

_____

If you hired a health and wellness professional, like a nutritionist or trainer, what would you expect them to look like? If you went to a fitness class, would you respect your teacher more if their body looked a certain way? How are these beliefs and biases perpetuating your own challenges around loving and accepting your body?

_____

_____

_____

_____

_____

_____

_____

_____

_____

_____

_____

_____

_____

_____

_____

Recall a time when you witnessed a judgment against someone else's body that didn't sit well with you. Why did this judgment feel wrong? How did it make you feel?

_____

_____

_____

_____

_____

_____

_____

_____

_____

_____

_____

_____

_____

ONLY I GET
TO DECIDE
HOW I FEEL
ABOUT MY
BODY, AND IN
THIS MOMENT,
I CHOOSE
PEACE.

Get Out of the Comparison Trap

Comparison often triggers addictive responses like impulse shopping, obsessively checking social media, self-shaming, people pleasing, and competition.

Write down your typical patterns when triggered by body-image comparison:

_____

_____

_____

_____

_____

Next, try this kundalini meditation for healing addictive patterns:

1. Come into a comfortable seated position, either cross-legged or in a chair, and close your eyes.

2. Make your hands into fists and extend your thumbs out. Place your thumb tips against the temples on the side of your head.

3. Silently repeat the mantra "Sa Ta Na Ma," signifying the end of a habit and the rebirth of a clear mind.

4. As you silently repeat each segment of the mantra, clench your molars together, and release during the silence. Keep your teeth together throughout. You will feel a slight massage on your temples. This elicits a neurological response that helps restore balance and clarity.

5. Try doing the meditation for one to three minutes.

Imagine how positively it would impact a child to see someone with a similar body shape, size, color, gender identity, or sexual orientation living life to the fullest! Write at least one action you can take that's out of your comfort zone when it comes to body image (like confidently wearing a swimsuit or certain style of clothing, or participating in a certain activity). What kind of ripple effect would you create in the world?

_____

_____

_____

_____

_____

_____

_____

_____

_____

_____

_____

_____

_____

Do you ever feel like you have to conform or hide part of yourself to be taken seriously or accepted? List the ways you feel pressured to cover, downplay, or enhance certain parts of your face or body to look more ideal. How would releasing the pressure of having to appear a certain way positively impact your life?

_____

_____

_____

_____

_____

_____

_____

_____

_____

_____

_____

_____

_____

Insecurities fueled by beauty standards or gender norms can often lead to us suppressing our natural tendencies and desires—for example, not ordering what we really want from the menu, selecting a more "appropriate" outfit, trying to cover up a visible disability, or opting out of an activity that sounded really fun. Think of a recent time when this happened for you. What beliefs were you upholding with these restrained choices?

_____

_____

_____

_____

_____

_____

_____

_____

_____

_____

_____

_____

_____

_____

NOT LONG AFTER TREATMENT FOR MY AUTOIMMUNE DISEASE BEGAN, I HAD A FULL-ON PANIC ATTACK. AND THE CRAZY THING IS, MY PANIC WASN'T INDUCED BY WHAT YOU'D THINK. NO, IT WASN'T THE SCARY DIAGNOSIS THAT CAUSED IT. I PANICKED BECAUSE THE POUNDS PACKED ON FASTER THAN I COULD BELIEVE. NEVER HAD I BEEN SO BIG. YEARS HAVE PASSED, AND I HAVE LEARNED HOW TO FIND PEACE WITH MY NEW SIZE. I REALIZE THAT THE SAME MEDS THAT ARE CAUSING MY WEIGHT GAIN ARE ALSO KEEPING ME ALIVE. I'VE DECIDED THAT INSTEAD OF FREAKING OUT ABOUT MY WEIGHT, I WILL EMBRACE THE FACT THAT I'M ALIVE. IF I HAVE TO CHOOSE BETWEEN LIVING AND BEING THIN, I CHOOSE LIFE.

— *Greta*

Reflect on any changes you want to make to your body, like weight loss, body modifications, or changing your hair. Are your reasons coming from a loving place, like wanting to support your body or expressing yourself in ways that feel fun and authentic, or does your motivation feel more like pressure? Finish this sentence for each change you'd like to make: I want to _____ because _____, and this makes me feel _____.

_____

_____

_____

_____

_____

_____

_____

_____

_____

_____

_____

_____

_____

_____

Write about 10 positive things you get to do, have, and experience with your body. Practicing an abundant mindset will lead to more feelings of fulfillment and inner peace!

_____

_____

_____

_____

_____

_____

_____

_____

_____

_____

_____

_____

_____

_____

The Power of Autonomy

The *APA Dictionary of Psychology* defines autonomy as "the experience of acting from choice, rather than feeling pressured to act," and it is considered a fundamental need that predicts well-being. Being around friends and family who are not on a body positive journey can pull you back into old ways of thinking. Close your eyes and imagine being in a conversation that feels like it's about to take a toxic turn. Instead of commiserating with the other person, what can you say or do to disengage from the conversation or get it back on a healthy track? Now, imagine yourself as a lighthouse for others who are also working to promote a more positive body image. How does it feel to lovingly support yourself and others around you?

How do you want to feel in your body? Let these words propel you forward in your body-acceptance journey. Invite your heart to speak now!

_____

_____

_____

_____

_____

_____

_____

_____

_____

_____

_____

_____

_____

It's no secret the media and pop culture show favoritism toward particular body types while marginalizing others. Think about stereotyped character roles for certain body types, the often-inaccurate representation or complete absence of disabled people, and the shaming and praising of celebrities for changes in their appearance. It's tough not to fall victim to media bias when it's literally everywhere, but you can break the trance! How has media bias shaped the way you think about your body and other body types?

_____

_____

_____

_____

_____

_____

_____

_____

_____

_____

_____

_____

_____

_____

_____

See It, Believe It, Be It!

For this exercise, you're going to make a vision board—with a twist! Rather than using images to envision a particular size or shape, your vision board will support you by representing your desired feelings. How do you want to feel in your body? Perhaps galloping horses invoke feelings of strength and power, whereas a warm sunset activates a sense of inner peace. Simply focus on the feelings you want more of and find pictures that bring out those feelings for you. Let this board serve as a visual reminder of the positive impact your body-acceptance journey will have on your life!

When you compare your entire life to someone's highlight reel, it's only natural that you may feel discouraged. Remember that you often don't see their whole story. Many people have their own struggles and insecurities around self-image. What words of support can you offer up to yourself when feeling triggered by comparison?

_____

_____

_____

_____

_____

_____

_____

_____

_____

_____

_____

_____

_____

_____

TO BE YOURSELF
IN A WORLD THAT IS
CONSTANTLY TRYING TO
MAKE YOU SOMETHING
ELSE IS THE GREATEST
ACCOMPLISHMENT.

— *Ralph Waldo Emerson*

Treating Yourself with Compassion

Truly loving your whole self, inside and out, doesn't happen overnight. Imagine unconditional self-acceptance as a garden that must be nurtured and attended to. Before your garden blossoms, you must first plant the seeds of self-respect and self-compassion, nurturing them with the gentle warmth of kindness, forgiveness, and grace. Daily, you will need to till the soil with awareness and healthy shifts. Through practice, you must learn how to lovingly uproot sensations of criticism, anger, and unworthiness as they sprout up. In this section you will be guided to sow the seeds of self-compassion, cultivating a deeper sense of harmony and balance in your life.

Compassion is the act of shifting criticism to kindness and judgment to understanding. Recall a recent judgment you made against your body. Then, finish this phrase: "My body deserves love and affection just as much as anyone else because . . ."

_____

_____

_____

_____

_____

_____

_____

_____

_____

_____

_____

_____

_____

_____

Think about a time when a person or even an animal extended compassion to you. How did it make you feel? How can you extend that same compassion to yourself on a daily basis?

_____

_____

_____

_____

_____

_____

_____

_____

_____

_____

_____

_____

_____

_____

MY BODY IS WORTHY OF LOVE, TENDERNESS, AND COMPASSION.

When in Doubt, Breathe It Out

Breathwork is an ancient and powerful healing tool that can lead to cathartic break-throughs around body image. The breath you will use is a simple inhale through a relaxed mouth, then an exhale through the mouth without forcing, letting the breath fall out. Make sure to bring the breath all the way down to the belly and feel it pass through the heart center. Create a playlist of three of your favorite uplifting songs. Find a space where you can lay comfortably on your back (or seated in whatever position is comfortable for you) and cozy up with a blanket. Turn on your playlist, close your eyes, and begin breathing in the style just described. When your playlist ends, place your hands over your heart, take one final deep breath, then gently sit up and reflect on your experience.

Perfectionism is a coping mechanism that people often use to make up for the things they don't like about themselves. Unfortunately, this constant chase can lead to even greater feelings of inadequacy and insecurity. Take some time to explore how perfectionism may be negatively impacting your life. Start by finishing this sentence: "When I obsess over changing my appearance and needing to be perfect, the real message I am sending to myself is . . ."

_____

_____

_____

_____

_____

_____

_____

_____

_____

_____

_____

_____

_____

When someone pays you a compliment, how do you respond? Do you believe them? Think about what your typical reactions say about your inner state of self-love and respect. Write about your reaction the last time you were paid a compliment. How do you think truly receiving a compliment would impact your mindset?

_____

_____

_____

_____

_____

_____

_____

_____

_____

_____

_____

_____

_____

_____

_____

A great way to practice and grow the skill of self-compassion is by pretending your body is someone you love and respect. Try it out! If your body were your best friend, how would you speak about it? Use this space to write about your body in the most loving way possible.

_____

_____

_____

_____

_____

_____

_____

_____

_____

_____

_____

_____

_____

WHEN I FEEL MY MIND LEANING INTO NEGATIVE THOUGHTS
ABOUT MY SHAPE, I REMEMBER THAT THIS IS A PRACTICE.
LOVING MYSELF IN ALL ITS MANY FORMS—BE THAT WEIGHT,
NUTRITION (OR LACK THEREOF), SHAPE, TONE—IS ALL VALID
AND PART OF MY SHORT JOURNEY HERE. SOME DAYS ARE
MUCH EASIER THAN OTHERS. I REMIND **MYSELF** THAT THIS
ORGANIC MEAT SACK IS JUST STARDUST REARRANGED. THAT
IT IS A TEMPORARY HOUSE. THAT I AM WORTHY AND A VALID
LIFE-FORM. THAT I AM MAGIC. IT WORKS MOST OF THE TIME.
AND IF NOT, I GO GET NACHOS BECAUSE . . . NACHOS.

—*Laurana*

Peace Begins with a Smile

Mother Teresa said, "Peace begins with a smile. Smile five times a day at someone you really don't want to smile at; do it for peace." It's time to apply this nurturing energy to yourself. Think of five places on your body to which you may have previously sent unkind thoughts. When you're ready, head to a mirror. Hold your gaze at each area while sending a loving smile to that part of your body. If you can't think of five parts, then simply alternate between different areas for a total of five times. Once you have completed five smiles, gaze into your eyes and offer up one last smile.

If your greatest insecurity could talk, what would it say? What would it want most from you? How can you support this insecurity with respect and kindness?

_____

_____

_____

_____

_____

_____

_____

_____

_____

_____

_____

_____

_____

_____

_____

_____

Compassion means meeting yourself where you're at. Forcing yourself into a state of total self-acceptance when it doesn't feel true will only backfire. Finish this sentence: "Although I don't love my . . ., I am willing to learn how to be at peace with it/them because . . ." Repeat this prompt for any areas or aspects of your body image with which you'd like to be more at peace.

_____

_____

_____

_____

_____

_____

_____

_____

_____

_____

_____

_____

_____

_____

_____

I AM
HONORED
TO BE THE
COMPASSIONATE
CARETAKER
OF MY BODY.

Journaling is an example of a healthy coping tool. By contrast, coping mechanisms like self-deprecation, extreme introversion, self-sabotage, and people pleasing can lead to greater feelings of frustration and angst. Have you ever used an unhealthy coping mechanism because of body dissatisfaction? How have these coping strategies impacted your life?

_____

_____

_____

_____

_____

_____

_____

_____

_____

_____

_____

_____

_____

Do you have goals for your body that cause anxiety or overwhelm, like reaching a number on the scale or achieving a certain look? Are you worried something bad may happen if you release this goal? (For instance, if I don't restrict my food, I will not lose weight; if I don't lose weight, then what?) It may feel a little scary to write out your fears, but once you see them, you'll discover if these goals still feel necessary!

_____

_____

_____

_____

_____

_____

_____

_____

_____

_____

_____

_____

_____

_____

_____

How would life be different if self-compassion was the guiding force? In such a life, what are you doing? Where are you? Who are you with? What experiences are you saying yes to? Go big and create a grand vision for yourself!

_____

_____

_____

_____

_____

_____

_____

_____

_____

_____

_____

_____

_____

Love Notes

It's likely that lots of the words you've directed toward your body haven't been too kind. And that's okay. But it's now time to shift the narrative. Your body craves your love, wanting nothing more than to be seen, loved, and tenderly held by you. Curl up in a cozy space, light a candle, put on your favorite uplifting song, then write a love letter to your body. Thank your body for all that it's done for you. Take some time to apologize to your body for the harsh words you've sent it. Let your body know your plans for your relationship moving forward. Let your pen flow. Your body is so ready to receive this sweetness and compassion from you!

_____

_____

_____

_____

_____

_____

_____

_____

_____

_____

_____

If body bashing is a learned behavior, then building yourself up can be learned, too! Practice building your body up by listing five things your body helped you do today. How would life feel if your body did not do these things for you?

_____

_____

_____

_____

_____

_____

_____

_____

_____

_____

_____

_____

_____

_____

TO SAY I'VE BEEN STRUGGLING WITH MY BODY THIS YEAR IS AN UNDERSTATEMENT. AFTER RECEIVING A SCARY DIAGNOSIS, I FELT LIKE MY BODY WAS QUITTING ON ME, AND THIS WAS TERRIFYING. YES, AUTOIMMUNE DISEASE IS CHRONIC, BUT MY LEVEL OF PAIN AND DISABILITY DOESN'T HAVE TO BE! THE ROAD TO HEALING HAS GIVEN ME THE **BIGGEST** SENSE OF GRATITUDE FOR MY BODY! I CAN OPEN A JAR! I CAN HOLD MY BABY! I CAN DO A CHILD'S POSE! I WILL SAY THAT STRUGGLING TO WIPE YOURSELF ON THE TOILET SURE GIVES PERSPECTIVE ON FINDING BODY LOVE! THE EXPECTATIONS OF MY BODY AND WISHES FOR ITS HEALING ARE SO SIMPLE THESE DAYS. LESS PAIN. BEING ABLE TO PUSH MY STROLLER AGAIN. AS A TEEN, I WAS A DANCER AND SUPER SKINNY, AND REALLY JUDGED MY BODY FOR HOW IT LOOKED. NOW, I'M JUST SO GRATEFUL THAT MY BODY WORKS. EACH MORNING I WAKE UP AND JUST THINK, WOW, I'M STILL HERE!

— *Abbi*

Has self-criticism closed you off from engaging in experiences, relationships, or opportunities that light you up? Has there been a recent invitation to do something fun or interesting that you declined, or are thinking about declining, because of how you feel about your body? How would it feel to release those feelings and shift them into excitement, or even neutrality?

Forgiveness is a huge step on the path of compassion. Are you ready to forgive yourself for the unkind words and actions you have engaged in? What can you forgive yourself for right now? Write it out and relish in the sweet release!

_____

_____

_____

_____

_____

_____

_____

_____

_____

_____

_____

_____

_____

_____

Reroute Yourself to Kindness

Neuroscience research suggests that people who write down their goals are more likely to achieve them. Creating a plan to overcome your daily challenges will help you achieve your goals—in this case, body acceptance! Using the following chart, create three daily reminders to support you through your typical self-love roadblocks. Divide your day into morning, afternoon, and evening. Within each of those segments, pinpoint a certain time when your body perception takes a dip (for example, dinner at 7:00 p.m., or scrolling social media around 2:30 p.m.). Then, fill in the chart with the following information to pair with your self-care reminder:

- An affirmation to lovingly get your mind back on track. Use one from this journal or create your own!

- One action item to do at that moment. Keep it simple and attainable, like deep breaths or listening to an uplifting song.

Once you complete the chart, set reminders in your phone or on your calendar for the week ahead!

	REMINDER TIME (e.g., 9:30 a.m.)	AFFIRMATION	ACTION
Morning			
Afternoon			
Evening			

Are you ready to extend forgiveness to those who may have contributed to your negative self-image? Forgiveness doesn't mean it was ever okay; it means you are moving on, no longer burdened by the pain, resentment, or grudges. Who are you ready to forgive now? How did this person impact your body perception, and how will forgiving them help you move on with your life?

_____

_____

_____

_____

_____

_____

_____

_____

_____

_____

_____

_____

_____

_____

Wearing uncomfortable clothing, denying your physical needs, and setting unrealistic expectations are examples of disrespect spurred by insecurities around body image and can result in feelings of anxiety, physical distress, and emotional turmoil. Self-respect is vital to your happiness and well-being! Write three ways you have disrespected your body. Then, write three ways you can respect and honor your wonderful body now.

_____

_____

_____

_____

_____

_____

_____

_____

_____

_____

_____

_____

_____

_____

Healing Touch

According to Dr. Kristin Neff, a leading researcher in the field of self-compassion, supportive touch "activates the care system and the parasympathetic nervous system to help us calm down and feel safe." Starting at the top of your head, place your hands directly on your body. Imagine warm healing energy or light moving from your hands to your body. Repeat the words "Thank you, I love you," as you move your hands down your body, resting them on the face, chest, belly, arms, hands, legs, feet, and anywhere else that calls to you. Listen to a playlist of two to three songs as you do this so you don't rush through it. How did it feel to send a loving touch to your body? Is this a practice you would like to come back to?

OUR WORDS HAVE
SO MUCH POWER.
EVERY DAY, IF YOU TELL
YOURSELF 'I LOVE YOU,'
IF YOU GIVE YOURSELF
ONE WORD OF
VALIDATION, IT WILL
CHANGE YOUR MIND.

— *Ashley Graham*

Embracing a Positive Mindset

The way you talk to yourself matters. Your inner dialogue paints your entire world, magnetizing experiences that match it. Research at the University of Lethbridge indicates that people who speak kindly to themselves are more likely to experience an uplifting and expansive life. A negative body image and critical self-talk typically go hand in hand. These habits can be learned as early as childhood, becoming so deeply ingrained that we believe they are just part of our personality. The good news is that you can take steps to unlearn these critical patterns and choose again. In this section you will journey into your inner world, transforming fear into love.

Renowned author and spiritual teacher Dr. Wayne Dyer said, "You'll see it when you believe it." When you look in the mirror, what kind of person do you want to see? Do you want to see someone who is burdened by self-doubt or radiating peace and joy? Write three or more positive thoughts this person has about their body.

_____

_____

_____

_____

_____

_____

_____

_____

_____

_____

_____

_____

_____

_____

_____

_____

What is the chief complaint you have about your body, the one thing you find yourself saying the most? Write three to five calming statements you can repeat when you feel this thought bubbling to the surface. Having these words prepared will help you cultivate a more positive mindset when you feel triggered.

_____

_____

_____

_____

_____

_____

_____

_____

_____

_____

_____

_____

_____

_____

_____

Feel It to Heal It

As reported by Dr. Alyson Stone, studies in neuroanatomy show that sitting with a feeling for at least 90 seconds will help you identify the source of the emotion and also release it from the body. Find an uplifting song that is at least 90 seconds long, close your eyes, and simply feel into your thoughts around your body image and self-worth. Invite any restrictive thoughts to make their way to the surface. You might consider: Do I feel worthy of happiness and abundance? What thoughts am I ready to release? What limiting loops or patterns am I ready to step out of? How have I attached my worth to my appearance? Once you find a question that surfaces an emotion, sit with it until you feel a sense of relief.

MY MIND IS PEACEFUL, MY BODY IS RADIANT, AND MY SOUL IS VIBRANT.

Today's narrative dictates that bodies deviating from the standard are considered flawed, when in reality, they're just different. And different is not bad! How does the word "flawed" make you feel in comparison to "different"? Which lens would you prefer to see yourself through?

_____

_____

_____

_____

_____

_____

_____

_____

_____

_____

_____

_____

_____

Visualize yourself upon waking, before getting out of bed. What can you say to yourself or do to start your day on a positive note? Something as simple as placing your hand on your heart and saying "Thank you" can make a big difference. Use the space provided to brainstorm and craft a simple, uplifting, and supportive morning ritual.

_____

_____

_____

_____

_____

_____

_____

_____

_____

_____

_____

_____

_____

_____

IT TOOK PREGNANCY AND POSTPARTUM TO TRULY UNDER-
STAND HOW TO LOVE AND ACCEPT MY BODY. PRIOR TO
PREGNANCY, I NEITHER LOVED NOR DISLIKED WHAT I LOOKED
LIKE, I SORT OF JUST WENT THROUGH LIFE WITHOUT A
RELATIONSHIP WITH MY PHYSICAL FORM. ONCE I BECAME
PREGNANT, I STARTED SERIOUSLY DISLIKING WHAT I SAW AND
STRESSED ABOUT MY EVER-CHANGING FORM. TODAY, MY
BODY IS HARDLY RECOGNIZABLE COMPARED TO WHAT IT WAS
BEFORE. A SOFT TUMMY, SAGGY THIGHS, BOOBS, AND BUTT.
AND YOU KNOW WHAT? I HAVE NEVER LOVED OR ADMIRED
THIS BODY MORE. I NO LONGER WORRY ABOUT BEING BACK
TO MY 'NORMAL.' INSTEAD, I GIVE MYSELF GRACE AND THANK
MY BODY DAILY FOR WHAT IT HAS DONE.

— *Sasha*

How does the voice of self-doubt, insecurity, or shame feel in your body? Is it a knot in your stomach or a tightness in your chest? The more you can recognize it, the easier it will become to call it out.

_____

_____

_____

_____

_____

_____

_____

_____

_____

_____

_____

_____

_____

Studies show that speaking positively to yourself impacts your mental and physical well-being. Write down an area of your body that you typically target with unkind thoughts. Next, write one kind statement about this area as though you were talking to it. Do this for as many body parts as you need to!

_____

_____

_____

_____

_____

_____

_____

_____

_____

_____

_____

_____

Your body-acceptance journey may be the breath of fresh air someone else desperately needs. How would you want someone struggling with comparison and body-image issues to feel if they came and sat beside you? What words of wisdom would you share with them?

_____

_____

_____

_____

_____

_____

_____

_____

_____

_____

_____

_____

_____

_____

_____

Mantra Love

Deepak Chopra, an internationally recognized leader in mindfulness, defines mantra as an instrument of the mind used to enter a deep state of meditation. Working with a mantra is an easy way to create more inner peace and is also a great remedy for the restless mind! In this exercise, you will pair the mantra "Peace begins with me" with hand movements, or mudras, for a multisensory approach to centering your mind.

Here are the mudras:

- Thumb to index finger: Peace

- Thumb to middle finger: Begins

- Thumb to ring finger: With

- Thumb to pinkie finger: Me

- Repeat

Even one minute of this meditation can bring relief. Try it for one to two minutes, then write three situations or places in which you can see yourself using this practice. The great thing about this meditation is that it's so discreet, no one will even realize you're doing it!

_____

_____

_____

_____

_____

_____

_____

A healthy ego helps keep you safe by alerting you to danger, but an unchecked ego tends to translate everything into danger (hello fear of rejection, self-doubt, and insecurity). A great tool for overcoming a powerful ego is calling it out and telling it who's boss. Use the space provided to lovingly tell your ego who is running the show and how things will look and feel from here on out. You get to be in the driver's seat, not your ego!

_____

_____

_____

_____

_____

_____

_____

_____

_____

_____

_____

_____

_____

Replace the negative words you often say about yourself with more uplifting coun-terparts by completing this sentence: "Instead of thinking I am too . . ., I choose to see that I am . . ." How will these shifts support a healthier mindset?

_____

_____

_____

_____

_____

_____

_____

_____

_____

_____

_____

_____

_____

_____

MY BODY
AND MIND
ARE FLOWING
WITH POSITIVE
ENERGY, AND
THAT ENERGY
IS FLOWING
BACK TO ME
TENFOLD.

Open Your Heart

Mindful movement isn't about burning calories or building muscle; it's simply about tuning in to your body and moving in a way that feels intuitive and supportive. Kundalini spinal flexes are a great way to activate the heart center and increase circulation to your brain.

1. Come to a comfortable seated position, either cross-legged or in a chair, with your feet planted firmly on the ground.

2. Place your hands on your knees, and inhale as you open your chest by lifting your chin and slightly arching your back.

3. On the exhale, bring your chin to your chest as you slightly tuck your tailbone.

4. Continue doing this for one to three minutes at a nurturing tempo, as you imagine your heart expanding and activating.

Tip: The breath is the heart of this exercise. If the full range of spinal movement is not available to you, simply place your hands in a comfortable position and inhale and exhale through the nose as vigorously as you can.

How did it feel to move your body in this slow, mindful way? List any other ideas of how you'd like to intentionally move your body.

_____

_____

_____

_____

_____

How do you think the world would change if we did away with society's idea of perfection and started seeing ourselves as perfect and whole, exactly as we are? What industries would go out of business?

_____

_____

_____

_____

_____

_____

_____

_____

_____

_____

_____

_____

_____

I'VE REALIZED THAT MY BODY IS NOT SOMETHING SEPARATE FROM ME AND THAT MY EMOTIONS AND FEELINGS EXIST INSIDE MY PHYSICAL BODY. TRUE EMBODIMENT IS ACKNOWLEDGING AND FEELING THE SENSATIONS, BOTH THE PLEASURE AND THE PAIN. RECOGNIZING THE MIND-BODY CONNECTION HAS BEEN SUCH A POWERFUL TOOL IN ALLOWING ME TO FEEL MY FEELINGS AND LIVE A MORE WHOLE AND INTEGRATED LIFE.

— *Jordan*

Body positivity can turn toxic when we feel pressured to love our bodies regardless of our true feelings. This is why we refer to body acceptance as a journey, not a final destination. Imagine the four points of the body positivity compass: self-respect, self-compassion, awareness, and joy. Now, recall a recent scenario when you felt bad about your body, and reflect on how you could have used one or more of these points to guide you back to your path.

_____

_____

_____

_____

_____

_____

_____

_____

_____

_____

_____

_____

_____

Imagine a mind free and clear of thoughts perpetuated by a negative body image. What other things could you spend time on if you weren't thinking about this?

_____

_____

_____

_____

_____

_____

_____

_____

_____

_____

_____

_____

_____

_____

_____

Become the Narrator of Your Life

Research shows that silently talking to yourself in the third person during a tough situation can help you feel more centered and confident. For example, instead of "Ugh, I look terrible," say "Sarah looks really nice." Try this out now. Think of a time your body image recently triggered you into feelings of self-doubt or criticism. Go back to the memory and narrate the story in the third person from a loving perspective, speaking about yourself as you would a best friend or someone you hold dear. In the space provided, write the story down. Then, record yourself telling the story. If you do not have access to a voice recorder, simply speak the story out loud. Close your eyes and listen as you speak. How did this new story make you feel in comparison to self-criticism? Next time you are going through a challenging situation, use third-person self-talk to shift out of discomfort.

_____

_____

_____

_____

_____

_____

_____

_____

_____

_____

Having healthy role models to serve as a source of inspiration can be so helpful when you are on a healing journey. Are there any people in your life who demonstrate a positive mindset? They could be a close friend, a family member, or even an influential figure you've never met. What do you admire about this person's mindset?

_____

_____

_____

_____

_____

_____

_____

_____

_____

_____

_____

_____

_____

_____

A 2017 article in *Psychology Today* explains that "cognitive distortions arise when our thoughts literally misrepresent the facts of what actually occurred." When this happens, your mind blows a situation out of proportion, leading to self-criticism and shame, when in reality everything was fine. Have you experienced cognitive distortion? What story was your insecurity telling? Was this story actually true, or was it your fear talking?

_____

_____

_____

_____

_____

_____

_____

_____

_____

_____

_____

_____

_____

_____

_____

One of the most powerful actions available to us on our healing journey is claiming responsibility for our own toxic traits. Get really honest with yourself: What behaviors and habits do you engage in that are not serving you or those you love?

_____

_____

_____

_____

_____

_____

_____

_____

_____

_____

_____

_____

_____

_____

_____

What's Your Love Language?

The five love languages is a concept created by best-selling author Dr. Gary Chapman and is based on the idea that everyone gives and receives love differently. Learning about one another's love language helps partners grow their relationship and build more solid foundations. Now, you get to take this same concept and apply it to yourself!

Think about the times when you feel really great because of something someone did for you. Use the list of the five love languages below and rank them in order of significance for you, with 1 being the least impactful and 5 being the most. After you have ranked them, write down a few ways you can show yourself love through the love language that resonates most with you. Next comes the fun part: Complete one of these actions now! Write about how it made you feel in the space provided. Come back to this list whenever you need a dose of self-love!

_____ Words of affirmation

_____ Acts of service

_____ Receiving gifts

_____ Quality time

_____ Physical touch

_____

_____

_____

_____

_____

BE YOURSELF.

LIFE IS PRECIOUS AS IT IS.

ALL THE ELEMENTS FOR

YOUR HAPPINESS ARE

ALREADY HERE. THERE IS

NO NEED TO RUN, STRIVE,

SEARCH, OR STRUGGLE.

JUST BE.

— *Thich Nhat Hanh*

Uncoupling Your Self-Worth from Your Body Image

You are so much more than a body! Your looks may change and weight may fluctuate, but your worth never will. You came to this earth to make a mark with your gifts and talents. Somewhere along the way you got so caught up in trying to squeeze your body into a certain standard that you forgot about your magnificent light and wavered from your worth. It's okay, though—you just took a detour. It's time to come home to your truest self now. In this section you will be gently guided to a space where you feel safe and excited to acknowledge and illuminate the wonderful facets of your entire being. It's time to meet your highest self!

SOME DAYS, MY PANTS FIT TOO TIGHT, MY SKIN LOOKS DULL IN A CERTAIN LIGHT, AND I FIND MYSELF CAUGHT IN A RELENT-LESS MENTAL LOOP OF SELF-HATE. IT IS ON THOSE DAYS THAT I AM FORCED TO PULL OUT EVERY TOOL IN MY TOOLBOX. EVEN THE DUSTY ONES AT THE BOTTOM. I LOOK AT MY EYES IN THE MIRROR AND REPEAT THE MANTRA 'I LOVE MYSELF.' I YANK OUT THAT QUOTE BY RUDY FRANCISCO THAT YANKS **ME** OUT OF MY FUNK, 'PERHAPS WE SHOULD LOVE OURSELVES SO FIERCELY, THAT WHEN OTHERS SEE US THEY KNOW EXACTLY HOW IT SHOULD BE DONE,' WHICH ALWAYS MAKES ME STAND A LITTLE TALLER. FEROCIOUS SELF-LOVE. THAT IS WHY WE'RE HERE.

— *Rosie*

Your self-concept, what you believe to be true about yourself, can be one of the most supportive or limiting belief systems you have. What do you believe to be true about you and your body? Do you believe you have the power to create an expansive life and mindset? Here are some words to help get you started: "I believe I am capable of . . ."

_____

_____

_____

_____

_____

_____

_____

_____

_____

_____

_____

_____

_____

_____

_____

_____

Why do YOU think so many people attach their self-worth to their outward appearance instead of their inner being? How has this story line impacted you?

_____

_____

_____

_____

_____

_____

_____

_____

_____

_____

_____

_____

_____

Shine Your Light!

When you stop seeking approval from others by acknowledging and appreciating yourself, your self-esteem flourishes and it becomes easier to live life on your own fulfilling terms. Using the chart below, acknowledge all the unique ways in which you shine! Under "My Light," write three to five attributes that you love about yourself; if that's too hard, think of things others have told you they like about you (e.g., funny, intelligent, kind). Then, in the second column, think of a story from your life when this attribute made you or those around you feel really good. You can just write down the name of the story, like "The time when I helped (a friend) move." Next, challenge yourself by reaching out to one to three close friends or family members and asking them to share stories and attributes that you can add to your list!

MY LIGHT	TIMES WHEN I SHINED

MY LIFE IS BRIMMING WITH WONDERFUL POSSIBILITIES, AND I AM WORTHY OF THEM ALL.

Oftentimes, our talents and strengths feel so natural that we may not even recognize them as gifts. A clue to your unique talents and strengths could be something your friends, family, or coworkers regularly come to you for. Make a list of 5 to 10 of your strengths and how each one makes you feel.

_____

_____

_____

_____

_____

_____

_____

_____

_____

_____

_____

_____

_____

_____

Your path is different from that of anyone else on this earth—your experiences and differences, the tough ones and the uplifting ones, have shaped you into the person you are today. Take some time to sit with this. How have your differences, physical and nonphysical, helped you become a better, more compassionate person?

_____

_____

_____

_____

_____

_____

_____

_____

_____

_____

_____

_____

_____

_____

_____

_____

How Can I Help?

Being of service to others is a really beautiful way to tune in to your life's purpose and can help you bust through your insecurities. Even if the act of service is only temporary, volunteering or offering a helping hand can elevate your mood and promote greater feelings of self-worth and connection. How can you help? In the space provided, brainstorm a few different activities to get involved in. What calls to you? Is there a population you'd like to serve and support? Come up with at least one activity you want to commit to and write it down; this can be anything from volunteering at a local shelter to carrying groceries for a neighbor to listening to a friend in need. Now, close your eyes and visualize yourself helping in this way. Afterward, write about how this visualization made you feel. Finally, make a commitment to yourself: When will you aim to actually do this?

_____

_____

_____

_____

_____

_____

_____

_____

_____

Think about a time, either recently or from childhood, when you felt totally "in the zone" without a care of what was going on around you. Maybe you even lost track of time. These moments are clues to when you are aligned with your highest self. What were you doing and how did it feel? How would your life change if you focused more on seeking this feeling rather than chasing an idealized body image?

_____

_____

_____

_____

_____

_____

_____

_____

_____

_____

_____

_____

_____

_____

Imagine your inner self shining through as the shadows of self-doubt fade away. Using your wildest imagination, describe your highest self. You can visualize your pure essence as a nonhuman form, like a brilliant light or color, or even an animal! Visit your inner sanctuary anytime you need to be reminded of your innate beauty.

_____

_____

_____

_____

_____

_____

_____

_____

_____

_____

_____

_____

_____

_____

_____

_____

_____

If someone were to ask your best friend or a loved one to describe you in the most loving way possible, what would they say?

_____

_____

_____

_____

_____

_____

_____

_____

_____

_____

_____

_____

_____

_____

_____

_____

Be Your Own Life Coach

Use the list below to score each facet of your life based on your level of satisfaction, with 1 being the lowest and 8 being the highest. After you rate each area of your life, take a look at the areas with the higher scores. What's going right? What strengths and belief systems are you utilizing in these areas of your life? These are proof points that you can, in fact, find meaning and happiness in your life. Next, take a look at the areas with the lower scores. Close your eyes and begin deep breathing. Invite your intuition to guide you. What changes would you like to make? How can you use your strengths to make these changes? Spend a few minutes here visualizing all the facets you need to support your growth and happiness. Afterward, write down anything that came up. Let your intuition guide you, and watch your life unfold in new and exciting ways!

_____ Health and well-being

_____ Career

_____ Finances

_____ Intimacy and romance

_____ Friendship

_____ Joyful experiences

_____ Home and physical surroundings

_____ Growth and self-development

_____

_____

_____

_____

_____

Is there a fear-based story from your past that you feel is blocking you from achieving your full potential? In what ways do you feel it has limited you? What would happen if you released it?

_____

_____

_____

_____

_____

_____

_____

_____

_____

_____

_____

_____

_____

Gratitude is the greatest currency for living a happier life. List as many things as you can about yourself and your life for which you are grateful.

_____

_____

_____

_____

_____

_____

_____

_____

_____

_____

_____

_____

_____

_____

_____

I NEVER KNEW WHAT IT WAS LIKE TO BE COMFORTABLE IN
MY SKIN UNTIL LATER IN LIFE. EVEN THOUGH I NEVER REALLY
STRUGGLED WITH ANY SIGNIFICANT CHALLENGES, I WAS CON-
STANTLY COMPARING MYSELF TO MY VERY SKINNY FRIENDS IN
A TIME WHEN THE WAIF LOOK WAS IN. I NEVER FELT GOOD
ENOUGH AND WAS ALWAYS IN MY HEAD. AND QUITE HON-
ESTLY, IT WAS EXHAUSTING. AS I GOT OLDER AND HAD KIDS, I
LEARNED TO APPRECIATE MY CURVES, AND EVEN THOUGH I'M
STILL SELF-CONSCIOUS OF CERTAIN PARTS OF MY BODY,
I'M PROUD OF HOW I LOOK. WHEN YOU LIVE LONG ENOUGH,
YOU LEARN TO REALIZE THAT WHAT SOCIETY DICTATES AS
ATTRACTIVE DOESN'T MATTER. I'VE LEARNED THAT TRUE BEAUTY
COMES FROM WISDOM AND BEING PROUD OF WHO YOU ARE.

— DeeDee

A question so many people grapple with is "Am I good enough?" Am I good enough to go for it, to say yes, and to live life on my own terms? Am I good enough to truly be seen for all that I am? It's time to take attention off these worries and highlight your worth. Why are you worthy of leading the life of your dreams? Why do you deserve all that life has to offer?

_____

_____

_____

_____

_____

_____

_____

_____

_____

_____

_____

_____

_____

_____

Write Your Power Statement

A power statement is a technique used in career counseling to help individuals concisely communicate their talents and achievements. In this exercise, you will create your own power statement to use as a tool to increase your confidence. Here's how to write your statement:

1. Write six attributes you admire about yourself. Then, circle the three that resonate the most.

_____

_____

_____

_____

_____

_____

2. Write three things you are committed to when it comes to your body-acceptance journey. Then, circle the one that aligns most with your vision.

_____

_____

_____

3. Create your statement using the following framework: "I, . . ., am a/an . . ., . . ., and . . . person who is committed to . . ." Here's an example: "I, Meg, am a kind, nurturing, and exuberant person who is committed to loving and accepting myself fully and unconditionally."

_____

_____

_____

_____

_____

Once you have created your power statement, head to the mirror and practice saying it out loud. Notice your posture as you speak, and invite your body to stand with confidence and ease. How does this statement feel in your body?

Is there a character trait you've been toning down or hiding, for fear of what others might think? How would it feel to unleash it? Why is this part of you just as worthy as the facets you already show to the world?

_____

_____

_____

_____

_____

_____

_____

_____

_____

_____

_____

_____

_____

_____

No one else is you—that is your superpower! Are you extra kind, super-intelligent, or wonderfully witty? List your superpowers. Then, finish this thought: "My superpowers positively impact the world by . . ."

_____

_____

_____

_____

_____

_____

_____

_____

_____

_____

_____

_____

_____

_____

It's Just Practice

Athletes practice their sport to hone their skills, and so can you! Cultivating a loving inner voice may take time, and that's okay! You wouldn't get frustrated with a kid who isn't amazing at soccer on their first day, right? This is why mindfulness is called a *practice*. In this exercise, you will strengthen the voice of love by practicing with it. Imagine your inner voice as a kind, wise, and compassionate guide. What does the voice of love sound like and feel like? This voice will be unique to you. Practice using this voice by starting with this: "Hi, it's me, your inner voice. I want to let you know . . ." Record your voice, then listen back. If you do not have access to a voice recorder, write down the words, then say them out loud slowly so you can feel into every word. How does this voice make you feel?

Purpose is often confused with a job title or specific role. But what if your true purpose was simply to find joy and live as the maximum expression of yourself? Visualize yourself living as the most YOU. How would it feel to live as the truest, highest version of yourself?

_____

_____

_____

_____

_____

_____

_____

_____

_____

_____

_____

_____

_____

_____

_____

_____

If money and body image were nonissues, how would you spend your time? Write about what lights you up and makes you feel really good on a soul level. Next, reflect on how you can create more opportunities to engage in these types of activities. Activate abundance and purpose by tuning in to your joy!

_____

_____

_____

_____

_____

_____

_____

_____

_____

_____

_____

_____

_____

_____

TODAY, I CHOOSE TO HONOR MY HIGHEST TRUTH AND FOLLOW THE PATH OF MY HIGHEST CALLING. WHEN I MOVE IN THIS WAY, I AM UNSTOPPABLE.

YOU ARE PERFECT.
TO THINK ANYTHING
LESS IS AS POINTLESS
AS A RIVER THINKING THAT
IT'S GOT TOO MANY
CURVES OR THAT IT MOVES
TOO SLOWLY OR THAT ITS
RAPIDS ARE TOO RAPID.

— *Jen Sincero*

Practicing Self-Care as a Form of Self-Love

Everyone deserves to feel free and happy in their bodies. And you, just as much as anyone else, deserve to live life on your own terms. Body positivity isn't a destination; rather, it is a journey made of daily choices. You get to decide how the journey will look and feel based on your unique needs and desires. What does self-care mean to you on a physical and emotional level? How can you support rather than suppress yourself? What would life feel like if self-care was your guiding force? In this section you will get clear on your needs and learn how to become your own advocate for self-care. Let's dive in!

I SUPPORT MY BODY IN WAYS THAT PROMOTE PEACE, JOY, AND TOTAL WELL-BEING.

An advocate supports and helps others in need, ensuring they feel heard, seen, and cared for. An advocate shares tools and knowledge that empower others so decision-making can be conducted from a place of clarity. How can you be your own self-care advocate?

_____

_____

_____

_____

_____

_____

_____

_____

_____

_____

_____

_____

_____

_____

_____

When you take time to care for your physical and mental well-being, you accomplish your goals with more ease and experience a greater sense of fulfillment. What does self-care look like to you? What are you doing? What do you no longer do?

_____

_____

_____

_____

_____

_____

_____

_____

_____

_____

_____

_____

_____

DEAR BODY, FOR YEARS I PUT YOU DOWN, SHAMED YOU. I THOUGHT YOU WEREN'T GOOD ENOUGH, ALWAYS ASKING FOR MORE. I WOULD TAN YOU, STARVE YOU, BINGE YOU, EXERCISE YOU, AND EVEN HATE YOU AT TIMES. I DREAMT OF A NEW YOU. A NEW FORM THAT I THOUGHT WAS PERFECT. I COMPARED YOU TO OTHERS, HOLDING YOU SO LOW THAT I DON'T KNOW HOW YOU GOT UP. FOR THIS I AM SORRY. I AM GRATEFUL FOR THE GIFTS YOU HAVE GIVEN ME, THE PLACES YOU HAVE TAKEN ME, AND YOUR STRENGTH EVEN WHEN PUSHED DOWN. NOW, I AM LISTENING. I HEAR AND HONOR YOUR CRAVINGS, NEEDS, AND WANTS. YOU ARE ONE AMAZING VESSEL, AND I HAVE LEARNED THAT WITHOUT YOU I COULD NOT DO THIS LIFE.

— *Sarah*

The Joy List

Write your top 10 ideas for self-care that invoke a sense of fun and play. Cuddling with loved ones (including furry friends), prepping colorful meals, dancing to your favorite song, or opening up the windows to feel sunlight and a fresh breeze on your skin are all lovely forms of self-care. Use this list as a reference when you want to raise your spirits. Feel free to keep the ideas flowing if you come up with more than 10. Next comes the fun part: Choose one activity from your list and try it now!

1. _____

2. _____

3. _____

4. _____

5. _____

6. _____

7. _____

8. _____

9. _____

10. _____

What does eating to nurture your body mean to you? Cultivate an abundant mindset by focusing on all that you will gain by eating in a more mindful way!

_____

_____

_____

_____

_____

_____

_____

_____

_____

_____

_____

_____

_____

How can you honor your body through movement and rest? What types of movement would you like to start or stop doing?

_____

_____

_____

_____

_____

_____

_____

_____

_____

_____

_____

_____

Visualize your most authentic self. How would you describe your personal style in a world where you don't feel like you need to look a certain way to please anyone? What kind of personal style feels most authentic to you?

_____

_____

_____

_____

_____

_____

_____

_____

_____

_____

_____

_____

_____

_____

_____

Self-Care Audit

It's time for a self-care audit. Write out your typical day from waking to bedtime. After you've described your day, feel into each part of it. Pay attention to energy black holes (such as skipped meals or lengthy screen time). Label each facet of your day as *draining*, *neutral*, or *enriching*. As you go through your audit, some questions to ask yourself are: Can I make this experience more mindful? Is there a way to change this experience to make it feel more nurturing? Is it necessary—can I skip it? Consider what you learned about the way you spend your time from doing this audit. What opportunities did you find for creating more pockets of time for care and ease? Now it's time to take action! Select one item you marked as *draining* and either cancel it or replace it with something new. There's no time like the present, so start now!

_____

_____

_____

_____

_____

_____

_____

_____

_____

Finish this sentence: "The thing I need most from family and friends when it comes to supporting my journey of self-acceptance and a positive body image is . . ."

_____

_____

_____

_____

_____

_____

_____

_____

_____

_____

_____

_____

_____

Take some time to define red flags that will alert you when you've fallen off your path of self-care. Examples of red flags could be a feeling that you are chasing an ideal image, engaging in activities that don't support you, or not honoring your needs and wants. What can you do when you notice a red flag?

_____

_____

_____

_____

_____

_____

_____

_____

_____

_____

_____

_____

_____

_____

I FULLY AND UNCONDITIONALLY LOVE AND RESPECT MY BODY, AND ANY CHANGES I MAKE ARE TO SERVE MY TRUEST SELF.

Putting your own needs last can be a hard habit to break, especially when you feel guilty for putting yourself first. But in time, it will get easier and become something you crave! What can you tell yourself when you feel guilty for engaging in acts of self-care?

_____

_____

_____

_____

_____

_____

_____

_____

_____

_____

_____

_____

_____

Not every act of self-care has to be a drawn-out affair. A deep breath with a hand placed on your heart or giving yourself a quick hug are small acts that make a big impact. In what ways can you give your body small moments of kindness?

_____

_____

_____

_____

_____

_____

_____

_____

_____

_____

_____

_____

_____

_____

I'VE REALIZED I WANT TO BECOME FRIENDS WITH MY BODY.
I WANT TO SAY HI TO EVERY PART OF IT AND THANK IT FOR
CARRYING AROUND THIS HEARTBEAT AND BREATH OF MINE.
IT WOULD FEEL SO MUCH NICER TO BE FRIENDS VERSUS ALL
THE CRITICIZING AND CRITIQUING. THANK YOU, BODY, FOR
YOUR PATIENCE WHILE I MADE PEACE WITH YOUR SIZE, SHAPE,
NOOKS, CRANNIES, AND NUANCES THAT DON'T ALWAYS FIT
INTO THE PICTURE-PERFECT MAGAZINE BUT CERTAINLY FIT JUST
RIGHTLY INTO MY WONDERFUL, IMPERFECTLY PERFECT TIME
HERE ON THIS PLANET. I'M SO GLAD WE ARE NOW FRIENDS.

— *Erika*

Are there any habits not serving your well-being that you are ready to quit, like scrolling late at night or snacking on junk food while watching TV? What healthy habits can you replace them with?

_____

_____

_____

Weave It In

Self-care doesn't have to be yet another obligation to add to your list. There are plenty of opportunities to create moments of self-care within your daily routine. All you have to do is align your actions with the intention of self-care. Try it with something as simple as drinking water. Fill a glass with fresh water. Next, set an intention that this moment is for you and your body. Thank the water for nurturing your body and supporting you. Take a sip mindfully and lovingly. Visualize the water moving through your body and enriching every fiber of your being. Close with a deep breath, filling yourself with gratitude. This can take as little as five seconds. How did this feel? What other activities can you bring this essence of intention to as a form of self-care?

_____

_____

_____

_____

_____

_____

_____

_____

_____

_____

_____

Reflect on the commitments you've attached yourself to that aren't serving your needs and priorities, especially around your body. Is there anything in your life right now that you can say no to or gracefully bow out of that you feel is not supporting your vision? Remember that saying no is a form of self-care, and you are allowed to change your mind!

_____

_____

_____

_____

_____

_____

_____

_____

_____

_____

_____

_____

_____

Write the names of any people in your social circle who you feel are toxic when it comes to supporting and promoting a healthy body image. Beside each person's name, jot down a boundary you can create to maintain a healthy distance. You are not obligated to tell this person about your new boundary; just know that it's there for you!

_____

_____

_____

_____

_____

_____

_____

_____

_____

_____

_____

_____

_____

_____

_____

Resource Yourself

Taking the time to create your own resource list will set you up for success when it comes to achieving your goals and feeling supported. It's time to do some research! Compile a list of local and online spaces that support your self-care vision. Ideas include wellness hubs and centers, organizations, studios, healthy grocery stores, farmers' markets and eateries, fitness centers, trails, parks, and community centers. Next, brainstorm authors, teachers, family, friends, and acquaintances who you feel would be a great addition to your body-acceptance journey. Finally, look for specific offerings, classes, meetups, or workshops in your local area and online that pique your interest. Record your research results here (use additional paper if needed). Then, select two to five options from your list that you will either visit or reach out to in the next few days.

_____

_____

_____

_____

_____

_____

_____

_____

_____

_____

_____

Finish this thought: "I feel like I'm supposed to wear . . ., but what I really want to wear is . . ." What thoughts and ideas are stopping you from dressing how you want? Can you challenge yourself to wear something that's been calling to you this week?

_____

_____

_____

_____

_____

_____

_____

_____

_____

_____

_____

_____

_____

If you've been interested in a new activity, like yoga, hiking, or cooking, go ahead and take the pressure of needing to be perfect off yourself now. Instead of perfection, try focusing on joy, empowerment, and community. How will you encourage yourself when trying something new?

_____

_____

_____

_____

_____

_____

_____

_____

_____

_____

_____

_____

_____

_____

_____

PRACTICING SELF-CARE AS A FORM OF SELF-LOVE

What does it mean to choose yourself? Moving forward, how can you commit to choosing yourself instead of succumbing to impossible beauty standards? Create a declaration of body acceptance by completing this thought: "I choose myself today and every day because . . ."

_____

_____

_____

_____

_____

_____

_____

_____

_____

_____

_____

_____

_____

_____

Dear You

Future-self writing is a fun way to hold yourself accountable while working with the Law of Attraction: When you concentrate your focus on your desired outcomes, you'll start to attract whatever you need to support that vision. As your future self, write a letter to your present-day self. Reflect on this pivotal point in your life—a time when you shifted into self-care and self-acceptance. What does your future self have to say about the strides you've made in body acceptance and how it impacted your life in a positive way? Once you've finished your letter, seal it in an envelope and store it in a special place. Then, mark one year from today on your calendar or planner as the day to open your letter.

Resources

TREATMENT OPTIONS AND ORGANIZATIONS

Casa Palmera: casapalmera.com/blog/body-image-therapy

National Association to Advance Fat Acceptance (NAAFA): naafa.org

National Eating Disorders Association: nationaleatingdisorders.org

The Body Positive: thebodypositive.org

The Body Image Therapy Center: thebodyimagecenter.com/issues-we-treat/body-image-self-esteem

Center for Change: centerforchange.com/treatment/types-of-therapy/body-image-therapy

The Body Is Not an Apology: thebodyisnotanapology.com

GLAAD Transgender Resources: glaad.org/transgender/resources

BOOKS

Beautiful You: A Daily Guide to Radical Self-Acceptance by Rosie Molinary

Big Girl: How I Gave Up Dieting and Got a Life by Kelsey Miller

Blind to Sameness: Sexpectations and the Social Construction of Male and Female Bodies by Asia Friedman

Body Respect: What Conventional Health Books Get Wrong, Leave Out, and Just Plain Fail to Understand about Weight by Linda Bacon, PhD, and Lucy Aphramor, PhD, RD

Embody: Learning to Love Your Unique Body (and Quiet That Critical Voice!) by Connie Sobczak

Looking Queer: Body Image and Identity in Lesbian, Bisexual, Gay, and Transgender Communities edited by Dawn Atkins

Oppression and the Body: Roots, Resistance, and Resolutions by Christine Caldwell and Lucia Bennett Leighton

The Pretty One: On Life, Pop Culture, Disability, and Other Reasons to Fall in Love with Me by Keah Brown

The Body Is Not an Apology: The Power of Radical Self-Love by Sonya Renee Taylor

Trans Bodies, Trans Selves: A Resource for the Transgender Community edited by Laura Erickson-Schroth

References

Broadwater, Ashley. "How to Be Body Positive without Being Ableist." *Ashley Broadwater* (blog). June 5, 2020. medium.com/@ashleybroadwater346/how-to-be -body-positive-without-being-ableist-cdebceb34b59.

Brown, Laura. "Being Precious: Gabourey Sidibe." *Harper's Bazaar.* January 7, 2010. harpersbazaar.com/celebrity/latest/news/a466/gabourey -sidibe-precious-interview-0210/.

Chapman, Gary D., and Amy Summers. *The Five Love Languages: How to Express Heartfelt Commitment to Your Mate.* Nashville, TN: LifeWay Press, 2005.

Chopra, Kamal. "Impact of Positive Self-Talk." Master's thesis, University of Lethbridge, Canada, 2012.

Cohen-Rottenberg, Rachel. "Where Are All the Disabled People in the Body Positivity Campaigns?" *The Body Is Not an Apology.* September 28, 2017. thebodyisnotanapology.com/magazine/where-are-all-the-disabled -people-in-the-body-positivity-campaigns.

Corporation for National and Community Service, Office of Research and Policy Development. *The Health Benefits of Volunteering: A Review of Recent Research.* Washington, DC: 2007.

Dyer, Wayne W. *You'll See It When You Believe It: The Way to Your Personal Transformation.* New York: Quill, 2001.

Emerson, Ralph Waldo. "Self-Reliance." *Essays: First Series, Volume II* in *Collected Works of Ralph Waldo Emerson*. Edited by Joseph Slater, Alfred R. Ferguson, and Jean Ferguson Carr. Cambridge, MA: Harvard University Press, 1979.

Feldman, Jamie. "Ashley Graham Is *The Edit*'s Last (and Best) Cover Star 2014." *Huffington Post.* December 31, 2014. huffpost.com/entry/ ashley-graham-the-edit-cover_n_6400442.

Hanh, Thich Nhat. *The Miracle of Mindfulness: An Introduction to the Practice of Meditation.* Boston, MA: Beacon Press, 1999.

Hay, Louise L. *You Can Heal Your Life.* Carlsbad, CA: Hay House, 1984.

Holland, Kimberly. "Positive Self-Talk: How Talking to Yourself Is a Good Thing." *Healthline.* October 17, 2018. healthline.com/health/positive-self-talk.

Moser, Jason S., Adrienne Dougherty, Whitney I. Mattson, Benjamin Katz, Tim P. Moran, Darwin Guevarra, Holly Shablack, et al. "Third-Person Self-Talk Facilitates Emotion Regulation without Engaging Cognitive Control: Converging Evidence from ERP and fMRI." *Scientific Reports* 7, no. 1, article no. 4519 (July 2017). doi:10.1038/s41598-017-04047-3.

Murphy, Mark. "Neuroscience Explains Why You Need to Write Down Your Goals If You Actually Want to Achieve Them." *Forbes.* April 15, 2018. forbes.com/sites/markmurphy/2018/04/15/neuroscience-explains-why-you-need-to-write-down-your-goals-if-you-actually-want-to-achieve-them.

Neff, Kristen. "Exercise 4: Supportive Touch." *Self-Compassion.* Accessed April 10, 2021. self-compassion.org/exercise-4-supportive-touch.

Sincero, Jen. *You Are a Badass: How to Stop Doubting Your Greatness and Start Living an Awesome Life.* Philadelphia, PA: Running Press, 2013.

Stone, Alyson. "90 Seconds to Emotional Resilience." *Alyson M. Stone* (blog). November 19, 2019. alysonmstone.com/90-seconds-to-emotional-resilience.

Thorp, Triss. "What Is a Mantra?" *Chopra.* January 14, 2021. chopra.com/articles/what-is-a-mantra.

VandenBos, Gary R., ed. *APA Dictionary of Psychology.* Washington, DC: American Psychological Association, 2007.

Weber, Jill P. "The Power of Your Internal Dialogue." *Psychology Today.* July 14, 2017. psychologytoday.com/us/blog/having-sex-wanting-intimacy/201707/the-power-your-internal-dialogue.

Acknowledgments

Thank you to my editor, Nora Spiegel, for your kindness and wisdom. I'm so grateful to everyone who contributed their words, time, and energy to the Real Talk segments in this journal. Justin, thank you for being an endless source of support, love, and comedic relief. You brighten my world, and I am deeply grateful for all the extra hours you spent being Superdad so I could write! Lily, Ruby, and Happy, thank you for helping me see my own beauty. Mom, thank you for modeling what it means to be a woman who stands in her truth. To my dad, who is no longer here on earth, thank you for guiding me throughout this process.

About the Author

 **MEGHAN SYLVESTER** is a dedicated practitioner and teacher of kundalini yoga and meditation, spiritual guide, and leader in the field of self-worth. Meghan brings a loving and nurturing energy to her experiences, making students of all levels feel comfortable and supported. She has led students all over the world in transformational experiences and retreats and continuously brings her wisdom of manifestation, meditation, and well-being to wellness publications, podcasts, and mindfulness-based events around the globe. As a passionate advocate for body positivity and vulnerability, Meghan openly shares about her insecurities and quest to embrace the softer side of life. Meghan is most proud of her roles as wife, mama, and friend. You can find her at MegSylvester.com or on Instagram at @MeghanSylvester, or tune in to her podcast, *Manifest Miracles*.